Tracing Black Music
To The Roots

By: Sharran C. Taylor

A.K.A. Poet Kween Yakini

Copyright © 2021
Original Work By Sharran C. Taylor
ISBN-13: 978-1-7323710-7-1

Disclaimer

The author has made every effort to provide a source of valuable information for the reader in this book and to provide information in regard to the subject matters covered. The author assumes no responsibility for errors, inaccuracies, omissions, or any other inconsistencies.

All Rights Reserved

No part of this book may be used or reproduced in any manner without written permission from the author except for use in review or articles.

Other Books By Sharran C. Taylor

Woke A Poetic Journey

Ode To The Punani: Sensual Rising

The Dream And The Lie

**In Loving Memory
Of My Beloved Queen Mother
Catherine Brabham**

(March 3, 1939 - January 8, 2022)

She was a gifted songbird
And a true lover of music!

THE AUTHOR'S NOTE

My wish for this collection of poetry is that it will uplift my readers by giving them more knowledge about the rich musical heritage that came out of the African Diaspora. In addition, I hope that I have made this book entertaining for you while sharing some background information about how our ancestors had a profound influence on American music and culture.

Certainly, Black people do have many exceptional achievements to be proud of but there is still much more to learn. Unfortunately for us there was a time when our history was purposely hidden from us, and many of us were led to believe that Black people did not matter and that we had nothing of significant value to offer this world. Thus, as a Black Poetry Writer I feel that it is my personal duty to take every opportunity possible to dispel any myths that remain about the supposed mediocrity of Africans and their descendants. And one thing I've learned from my ancestors is that giving up is never an option for us and that we are more than capable of rising above any obstacle we face.

Of course, I'm aware that it will take generations to sweep away the delusions of the past that have plagued us for centuries, but I also know that the more we continue to write our own narratives the less we'll be defined others. So, writers must do more to unveil the hidden parts of our history so that we can never again become blind to our own greatness.

TABLE OF CONTENTS

Introduction……………………………………..……..1

The History Of The "Ngoni" And The "Banjo ………3

That Old Banjo…………………………………………..5

The History of the "Djembe"……………………..11

The Sound Of The Drums………………………..13

The History Of Negro Spirituals………………………20

The Essence Of Gospel…………………………….22

The History Of Blues……………………………….28

We Know All About The Blues……………………….30

The History Of Jazz…………………………………..35

The School Of Jazz………………………………....37

The History Of "Rock And Roll"………………………43

The True Legends Of Rock And Roll…………………45

The History Of The Afro-Latino Infusion……….....50

The Afro-Latino Infusion………………………………52

The History Of Civil Rights……………………………………55

Music Of The Movement………………………………………..57

The Legendary Nina Simone…………………………………..64

The Power Of Nina's Blues……………………………………..66

The History Of R&B………………………………………………72

For The Love Of R&B……………………………………………74

The History Of Hip Hop………………………………………...81

NYC Mic Checker…………………………………………….....83

Why I Love Hip Hop…………………………………………….88

The History Of Black Music Creatives…………………..98

The Black Creatives………………………………….........101

Ways That You Can Support An Artist or Author …...109

Black Music History Q & A………………………….....110

Works Cited……………………………………………….....111

INTRODUCTION
"Tracing Black Music To The Roots"
By: Sharran C. Taylor

Black music can easily be traced back to Africa when we look at some of the cultural traditions that were implemented in the creation of the Black music genres of today. When you listen closely to the traits and rhythm in Black music you can easily identify distinct elements that are rooted in ancient African techniques such as *"Call and Response"* that was originally developed by the "Griots" and "Jales" of West Africa. Even today those same prominent individuals still hold significant status in African culture as being the historians, storytellers, praise singers, poets, and musicians who are the keepers of African oral tradition. Therefore, it is unquestionable that people of African descent carried their valuable musical heritage with them to the "New World" which has become the base of North, South and Central American music cultures. And I am confident that *"Tracing Black Music To The Roots"* will illustrate how our African ancestors and their descendants have played a pivotal role in American music culture and others around the world.

Still today, some may not know that Black musicians have actually been drawing upon their ancestral connections to help create all of this great music that we all love. And after close examination it's undeniable that our African heritage was indeed the common thread that helped spark our creative abilities in America. This connection also explains how our enslaved ancestors, who were falsely said to be unteachable, were intuitively able to produce Negro Spirituals and Work Songs that helped them make it through those long and exhausting workdays in the hot sun. In addition, those early work songs would later provide the foundation for Gospel, Blues and other music genres.

Given these historical facts, it's clear that the link that we continue to have to our African roots has been the key that has allowed us to create some of the most amazing music that the world has known. Furthermore, because of the "Atlantic Slave Trade" and the "African Diaspora" that occurred in so many different places, African music culture would also have a profound influence on Caribbean and Latin music genres as well. I sincerely hope that *"Tracing Black Music To The Roots"* will in some way shine the light on some hidden sections of our history and may it also give the proper credit to an African heritage that was so powerful that it literally transformed music across all racial and ethnic backgrounds around the world. Cause' at the end of the day, if it had not been for the strength and resilience of Africans and their descendants, American music and culture wouldn't even come close to what it looks or sounds like today.

THE HISTORY OF THE "NGONI" AND THE "BANJO"

(Created in the 13th century in the villages of West Africa)

The *"Ngoni"* is an ancient African musical instrument that is said to be the great ancestor of the Banjo. The body of the *Ngoni* is made from a long, thin, hollow piece of wood with leather stretched on it, resembling a drum. The long, straight neck is inserted into the body that does not quite extend the length of the body. The strings are made of fishing line stretched just past a small opening in the face to a bridge at the base of the body. The strings are held in place by thin leather strips, which can be moved up and down the neck to change the tuning. Like the tuning, the number of strings and size of the instrument can vary greatly. When plucked, the Ngoni makes a deep resonating sound.

This instrument originated in West Africa, and it's part of the *Mandinka* culture. People who identify with this culture are also known as Mandingo, and they live throughout Africa, maintaining their origins with the *Mali Empire*. West African storytellers called *"Griots"* have used this instrument to accompany the narrations of their history since the 12th century.

The beloved instrument never made the journey on the slave ships bound for the Americas, but the technology for building them was carried in the heads of the passengers along with their memories of the music. Generations later the enslaved Africans would make variations of those instruments in the fields of the Mississippi Delta and elsewhere thereby continuing its legacy through the evolution of the American Banjo.

However, during in the 1800s, the minstrel shows would become a popular form of entertainment for White people, where they would perform in blackface as they would play the Banjo while sang and danced in a caricature of Black music and culture.

But today we are reclaiming the history of the Banjo and making it clear that this instrument, that is so central to American cultural, is in fact part of African culture.

That Old Banjo

It was sweet the sound of the Ngoni
That gave our people some kind of peace
Recalling our history and oral traditions
That were taught by the Griots and the Jeli!

We recalled their songs of praise for our Ancestors
Those were good memories for us to keep
As we laid sick and dying on slave ships
With shackles on our hands and feet!

So, even if our bodies were maimed
Or we were crippled by all of the pain
Our minds, would never forget the land
From which the old Banjo came!

Yes, we were stolen from Africa
But we still carried traditions from our homes
And the enslaved Africans recreated the Ngoni
So, that they would never feel alone!

You see that Old Banjo didn't come from
No men with white faces!

It was made by West Africans
From past generations
The original was created far, far away
From these old and rotten plantations
Were we had Kings and Queens
Who ruled early civilizations

We were historians, poets and musicians
Singers, craftsmen, and engineers
Not some ignorant savages
Running around naked with spears
We were the descendants of Mali
And our Griots were unquestionably revered!

So, the original Banjo was made by enlightened men
Not some three fifths of a man they called a slave
Yet some still deny our humanity
Despite all of the contributions that we've made

Yes, they've appropriated our music
But no credit or recognition was bestowed
Instead, we were insulted by racists satire shows
Where they mocked our people and their beloved Banjo

White people sang songs like "Mammy"
They offended us by wearing blackface
As a result, we began turning away
And viewing the Banjo as a disgrace

Yet African's still had an influence on the music
You can hear it whenever Blue Grass music is played
Believe me if it wasn't for the sound of the Banjo
American Folk music wouldn't even sound the same

Now I read somewhere that
Some White folks tried to claim credit
For that Old Banjo
But they can't whitewash our history
Like we didn't descend from great souls

So, it's time to embrace the truth
And cast away those delusions and fears
Cause' Black folks have been shaping musical cultures
For more than 400 years

Now, we know some things have changed
And we're no longer bound to any ships

But just look at how we're still struggling
To reclaim our rights and cultural ownerships

Yes, they may love our music
But many still don't have a clue
That Black folks have had to fight for recognition
Even when the credit was rightfully due

That's why those sins of the past
Have to be corrected!
For even today we continue to see that
Black lives are still being disrespected!

So, we must let it forever be known
That the Banjo was derived from an African creation
It's time that we were recognized for our greatness
Time to give Black people more appreciation
Because it was our ancestors who brought
The blueprint for the Ngoni
Despite all of the trauma and humiliation

So, today let us reflect on this:
During a time of mass social awakening
That we are finally having a real conversation

About the hidden parts of the American population
Because inside the music there lies an African foundation

And let us be proud of the success we've had
Through our cultural integration
Maybe music can be the means
To bring about a necessary reconciliation

You see, music is like food or language
Cause' it truly has a flowing spirit
Yes, it has many ethnic influences
But it's up to us to stop and hear it!

Our cultures are incredibly intertwined
America has become a nation of sisters and brothers
But you must also respect the African culture
That binds us to one another

Remember it was the sweet sound of the Ngoni
That gave our people some kind of peace
Recalling our history and oral traditions
That were taught by the Griots and the Jeli!

We recalled their songs of praise for our Ancestors
Those were good memories for us to keep
As we laid sick and dying on slave ships
With shackles on our hands and feet!

So, even if our bodies were maimed
Or we were crippled by all of the pain
Our minds, would never forget the land
From which the original Banjo came!

THE HISTORY OF THE "DJEMBE"

(12ᵗʰ – 13ᵗʰ Century)
The Djembe comes from the villages of West Africa

The *Djembe*, also known as the drums, is one of West Africa's best known instruments. There are at least a dozen stories on the history of the drums, told by many master drummers. The djembe drum is most likely about 400-800 years old and was created during the Malian Empire by the Mandé people. This goblet-shaped drum is traditionally carved from a single piece of African hardwood and topped with an animal skin as a drumhead.

It is taught that Blacksmiths made the first djembes, making each drum custom-fitted to the drummer who would play it. The making of the drum was a spiritual undertaking. The blacksmith would be the one to cut down the chosen tree and was obliged to make offerings and give thanks to the spirits for the trees he cut down. After the tree was selected, a sacrifice would be made to ask for permission to cut the tree for a djembe. Once the blacksmith finished the djembe, it was delivered to the drummer who commissioned it, a member of the *jeli caste*. *The jeli* are musicians, who are responsible for the oral history of their people, and this remains true to today.

Traditionally, only those born into the djembe family would be allowed (or interested) to play the djembe. Castes have last names that have survived to this day and if your last name (your family name) is one of those families born into the djembe, it is your instrument and possibly your job to play the drum for the village.

Our Africans ancestors say that the drum contains three spirits. The first spirit comes from the tree from which it was made, the next spirit comes from the animal whose skin is played, and the last spirit is from the carver who cut the tree and assembled the drum. We would add that possibly the most important is the spirit of the ancestors. I have seen the oldest djembe known today and it has the names of generations of djembe masters from many countries and villages.

The Sound Of The Drums

They say there once was a time
    When we learned our History
    From the West African Griots and the Jeli
    Who would play the Djembe for their people
    By the way Djembe means Drums
And the Jeli musicians, would recite
    The oral history of their people
    So, this was serious business
    They didn't do it just for fun
That's why this is a heritage
    That we must know my beloved ones
This is something you must understand
    For you are the descendants of Africans
    Daughters and Sons
And you can't truly comprehend who you are
    Until you know where you came from
That's why we must give thanks to the Jeli
    For passing down the gift of these Drums!

So, don't you ever let your ears neglect
This indigenous dialect
That's infused with a telepathy that's so spectacular

Learn the ancient history of this rhythmic vernacular
That's like a disseminated speech
That is manifested by the drums that we beat
Cause' we be killing these drums!
Using all of our fingers
And changing the tempo with our thumbs
Pounding away, until our flesh becomes numb
So, you better listen, listen!
Cause' there's a message in these drums!

Listen to the way we emphasize
The sounds of celebration
These drums are the connectors
They bid you salutations
Oh yeah, we've been doing this
For countless generations
So, you need to thank these drums
Because they gave us the right foundation
Without the drums there would be no Hip Hop Nation!
And we wouldn't have no real jamz playing
On those Radio Stations!

So, go ahead and give us that drumroll please
And let us "Dance To The Drummers Beat"

Give us those crashing cymbals
The Base and the snare
It's time to let the Drummer
To takes us there!

You see how we respond
To that dynamic rhythm
Cause' we don't just
Hit'em and Hit'em
We Live'em and Live'em
And dig into that rhythm
Like it's some kind of hypnotism
From Hip Hop to Jazz and Be Bop
Soul is what we give'em!

Look, I'm just saying!
Black music be slaying
Once that beat takes control
The hips just start swaying
It's like catching the spirit
Maybe it's time to start praying
Listen, we came to dance all night long
So, somebody better start playing!

So, let's have a rhythmic conversation
Give us that re-mix variation
Bless us with those jazzy textures and tones
That leads to an outburst of gyration
And watch those drums take us
To a higher elevation!

It's that base and that rhythm
That helped musicians to synchronize
But you know how Black folks do
We had to go and improvise
And with the gift of our heritage
We created Jazz, The Blues
And all that other Jive

Can't you feel it?
Now you're catching the vibe!
But it's also important for us to realize
What these drums really symbolize
For, within our history and culture
Is where the absolute truth lies

But you gotta differentiate the sounds
Cause' these drums are more than cool

They can speak to our souls
Like spiritual tools
Connecting us back to our roots
Like subliminal jewels

Listen, this flows straight from our hearts
So, it never needs to be scripted
Because the beat of these drums
Are divinely encrypted
And the drummers hands are supremely gifted
With the drive to keep our people uplifted

And believe me I ain't bluffin
Cause' these ain't just any percussions
That we're discussing
These are the sounds of our distant
But never forgotten cousins!

These drums take us back
To the rivers of the Congo
Where the ancestors called them bongos
Today's these musical aficionados
Can play them with a whole lot of bravado
But we've been played these drums

Since we lived among the Africanos
We even played them on plantations
When our voices were incommunicado
Then we took them from the Cotton Club
To Motown and straight to the Apollo

Because there once was a time
    When we learned our History
    From the West African Griots and the Jeli
    Who would play the Djembe for their people
    By the way Djembe means Drums
And the Jeli musicians, would recite
    The oral history of their people
    So, this was serious business
    They didn't do it just for fun
That's why this is a heritage
    That we must know my beloved ones
This is something you must understand
    For you are the descendants of Africans
    Daughters and Sons
And you can't truly comprehend who you are
    Until you know where you came from
That's why we must give thanks to the Jeli
    For passing down the gift of these Drums!

THE HISTORY OF NEGRO SPIRITUALS
(Spirituals began in 1619 – 1700)

The origins of gospel music began during the slavery period in America. It was then that the enslaved Africans would create Negro spirituals which they created to pass on hidden messages. For example, when Harriet Tubman was nearby, slaves would sing "Go Down, Moses" to signify that a 'deliverer' was nearby. Our ancestors were so clever that, they created songs with hidden meanings using the only text that they were allowed to have, the Bible.

Negro Spirituals would later influence Gospel music, and Gospel music would come to have a profound influence on all genres of music. As Gospel artists would become inspired by pop music, which would impact early Rhythm and Blues artists, while other Gospel artists would also have an effect on the creation of Soul music by bringing gospel inspired harmonies and traditions from rhythm and blues.

And as our music would continue to evolve, music groups would base their music on songs they had been singing in church, which would later create gospel songs that were altered for secular audiences.

Even the underlying features of Soul/R&B music would influence Gospel artists who would incorporate secular music styles into their music. Additionally, the secular songwriters would incorporate gospel songs into their music as well.

The Essence Of Gospel

Negro Spirituals may have been created
By using some Biblical texts
But the songs weren't just about scriptures
They were signal songs that told runaways
What they had to do next

Certainly, they gave us hope
When we were lost and depressed
But the lyrics were actually about
Finding the Underground Railroad
And their original purpose
Was meant to guide and to protect

The early songs were easy to code
So, our Ancestors used them on plantations
Cause' we're good at taking what's been given
To create our own positive affirmations
They were able to conceive spiritual songs
To help carry them beyond their dire situations
That's how they endured those long hot days
Until their freedom became a manifestation

Spiritual songs gave our enslaved ancestors
A way to express their solidarity
They sang songs about receiving their freedom
And the messages were received with clarity

But those crafty old songs
Were encoded with specific directions
They helped them to plan their escape
By breaking the songs down into sections

Spirituals songs are ingrained in our heritage
That's why they are worthy of our reflection
As we've passed them down for generations
To give us a sense of family and connection

And that Negro spiritual "Wade in the Water"
Told them if you hide in the river
Then you'll make it through
When the runaways heard this song
They knew exactly what they had to do

But, in the song "Swing Low, Sweet Chariot"
"Swing low" meant they were taking
The enslaved to the North

While "Sweet Chariot" was telling them
That "The Underground Railroad"
Will be the transportation source

It's been said that Harriet Tubman
Used to sing spirituals
To signal her presence to those who wanted to escape
So, the song "Steal Away" made them aware
That they were planning a freedom break

And Gospel music is also derived from
An African cultural foundation
The technique that they used was
"Call and Response" improvisation
Our ancestors relied upon African culture
To provide a secret type of communication
And eventually those old Negro spirituals
Would also become the basis
Of Gospel, Blues, Jazz and
Other types of music genre formations

But today Gospel is called church music
And the music genres seem so separated
Some say that secular music is sinful

Because Black music history has faded
That's why we need to dig into the roots
And the journals need to be reevaluated
Cause' if we look at the past
The evidence is quite overstated

Yes, there are some conceptual differences
But, Spirituals, Gospel and the Blues
Are closely related
Without the infusion of Black music genres
"We Never Would Have Made It"

Listen, Gospel music and the Blues is mutual
Yet they both have their own distinct characteristics
A gospel song can easily become a blues or soul song
Just by changing a few words that are genre specific

Songs like "Take My Hand, Precious Lord"
Was written by *Thomas A. Dorsey*
Who was a Gospel, Jazz and Blues musician
And he created some great Gospel Blues songs
That made folks wanna stand up and listen

Because all of the music that we create
Has similar musical origins and traits
Black artists influenced many different cultures
And they did it with such "Amazing Grace"

Yes, we all love Black Music
But have you ever question the roots
Cause' many don't see the connection
So, I came to provide some proof

So, "Let Us Break Bread Together"
For we've all gone "Down in the River to Pray"
Remember if it wasn't for our Ancestors
We wouldn't have the music that we all enjoy today

And this is "Why We Sing"
Cause' we can see "A Brighter Day"
And no, the fight isn't over
But we know in our spirit it's gonna be okay

That's why Edwin Hawkins sang "Oh Happy Day"!
And Kirk Franklin just made you wanna "Stomp"!
Cause now we're "Free at last", "Free at last"
And don't this music make you wanna "Stomp"!

This is why we must never forget
The reason why those spirituals were made
Those songs had a dual meaning for us
So, all black music must be maintained

Remember, Negro Spirituals may have been created
By using some Biblical texts
But the songs weren't just about scriptures
They were signal songs that told runaways
What they had to do next

Certainly, they gave us hope
When we were lost and depressed
But the lyrics were actually about
Finding the Underground Railroad
And their original purpose
Was meant to guide and to protect

THE HISTORY OF "BLUES"
Blues began in the 13ᵗʰ century
In the villages of West Africa

The origins of the *Blues* came from West Africa, and one could also say that the word itself seems to define the journey of the *African Diaspora* to the new world. Unquestionably, the true beginnings of the *Blues* can be traced back to the culture and musical traditions of the West African *Griots* and story tellers who had the responsibility of preserving their history through oral traditions. Thus, that legacy was continued by Black American Artist and musicians who used their ancestral ties to create some of the most groundbreaking music in American History. For example, it was our African influences that contributed to the creation of *"work songs"* when we used musical arrangements such as *"call-and-response"* that was performed by the field hollers and workers, as well as the spiritual chants and rhymed narrative ballads that led to the creation of *Negro spirituals*. But it was those African customs and those early music compositions that were later infused with the artistic vocal style of the American Blues

I would say that Negro Spirituals was the parent of the American Blues and Gospel music, and they became the parents of many other sub genres like Jazz, R&B, Country, Soul, Rock and Roll and Hip Hop. Blues are Gospel are like two siblings and both genres of have always been very popular in Black community. In fact, it would be the fusion of many music styles that would eventually lay the groundwork for Hip Hop music which would become the Great, Great Grand Child of the previous genres that would be conceived in the mid-1970s.

History would later show that in the 20th century, Black American music would be responsible for the growth and popularity of American music and culture. And as a result, of the contributions and creative talents of Black Americans, America would be recognized as the home of some of the most influential musicians that the world had ever known.

We Know All About The Blues

The Blues ain't nothing new to us!
Cause' we've been telling the Blues
Since West African Griots began
Recounting the past of our people
Through oral traditions
For centuries we've shared our history
Utilizing poetry, songs and spoken word exhibitions

And when we combined those traditions
With the musical sounds of the Ngoni
We tapped into the basics of the Blues
So, Black Americans didn't need to be born in Africa
Because Africa lives in our womb!

That's why our destiny for greatness
Was already set in motion
And those disrespectful chains
Were inevitably broken
Because the arms of Mother Africa
Can surpass any ocean

But they say that the Blues
Was born in the South
Similar to Artist like BB King
Who was born on a plantation
He loved his guitar so much
That Blues Music became his true salvation

Our Folks played the Blues at house parties
And social gatherings for recreation
They created that real down home sound
Through practice sessions and collaborations

Legends like Louis Armstrong created scatting
It was a singing technique that was crazy-cool
And he taught this skill to other Blues artists
So, they could alter a song's lyrics to suit their moods
And this singing style was like an African chant
Which just added another layer to our vocal tools

But you can't just sing a Blues song
It's something you have to feel
In the deepest part of your soul
Cause' when a Blues singer hit's the mic
Believe me it's a spectacular sight to behold

Go and listen to the distinguished vocals of
Sarah Vaughan
Bessie Smith
Ella Fitzgerald and Etta James
Yes, they all sang the Blues
But they each had their own lane
And they made it look so easy
Cause' their skill levels were insane
They were considered world class singers
That's why we must never forget their names

Like I said we know all about the Blues!
Cause' we don't just write and sing the Blues
We exemplify and live the Blues
And that's why we had artist like Ma Rainey
Who gave us that old "Black Bottom" Blues
Oh please, trust and believe
That our brothers had some
Exceptional vocal talents too
Remember that Muddy Waters
Bo Diddley and Ray Charles
Blessed us with some outstanding tunes!

But if we're talking about Black legends

Then you gotta listen to some Billie Holliday Blues!
Cause' Billie had that "Strange Fruits" kind of Blues
And Billie sure made them White folks mad
When she stood up there and sang that tune
But she also gave us that
"God Bless The Child" kind of Blues
And sometimes she would touch our souls
With that "Good Morning Heart Ache" type of Blues!

You see, Black music creativity
Is like a pot of gumbo
That just keeps on stewing
So no, we ain't done
Cause' we're always improving
From West Africa
To the jive joints of Harlem
We keep creating and moving
We are the trailblazers of music
So, ain't no way we could ever be losing

Although we've faced many obstacles
We are definitely the music trend setters
Our music is transformative and groundbreaking
And that's why we deserve all that cheddar

For that moe better!

But world music wouldn't be what it is today
Without Black music creatives
If you really wanna know the truth
Cause' genres like Rock and Roll, Jazz and others
Are the fusions of our melodic fruits
Although, our tree has many branches
The Blues will always be the root

Remember, the Blues ain't nothing new to us!
Cause' we've been telling the Blues
Since West African Griots began
Recounting the past of our people
Through oral traditions
For centuries we've shared our history
Utilizing poetry, songs and spoken word exhibitions

And when we combined those traditions
With the musical sounds of the Ngoni
We tapped into the basics of the Blues
So, Black Americans didn't have to be born in Africa
Because Africa lives in our womb

THE HISTORY OF JAZZ

*(Jazz began in New Orleans during the early 1900's)
This was also during the
"Harlem Renaissance" period of the 1920's*

The enslaved who were taken from West Africa brought some rich musical traditions which continued in the songs and field chants of African descendants. When slavery was abolished and the American Civil War ended (1865), many former slaves found jobs as musicians, exposing them to other musical styles from around the world.

From 1920's to the 1930's, the great migration of Black people from the rural South to the urban North sparked an African American cultural renaissance that became known as the Harlem Renaissance. This movement marked the first time that mainstream publishers and critics turned their attention seriously to the Literature, Music, Art and Politics of African descendants. It was during that era that Jazz was born in New Orleans. Music from all over the world could be heard on the streets of New Orleans and was also one of the only places in America that permitted the formerly enslaved Africans to retain their heritage of the drums.

Jazz music began to trickle into American music and eventually it erupted out of the streets Harlem and then into Black nightclubs that offered illegal liquor and great dancing. Jazz started becoming a great draw for not only Harlem residents, but outside white audiences also. Some of the most celebrated names in American music regularly performed in Harlem: Louis Armstrong, Duke Ellington, Bessie Smith, Fats Waller and Cab Calloway, often accompanied by elaborate floor shows. Tap dancers like John Bubbles and Bill "Bojangles" Robinson were also popular.

Because of the birth of Jazz and the Harlem Renaissance, African American artists, writers and musicians were able have control over how the Black experience was represented in American culture and set the stage for the civil rights movement.

The School Of Jazz

Listen, to me man!
If you wanna go to
The Scholl of Jazz
You don't need to be
No college Grad
But you do need to have some chops
And a whole lotta pizzazz
You gotta know how to talk that Jive
And get with the lingo man!
And keep those joints jumping
For those jitterbug fans!

Now listen to me Daddy-O,
It don't matter if your name is
Lucky Sam
Or
Shy Abraham
All they hear is
Yes, Sir!
Yes Ma'am!
Hot diggity damn
Those cats are playing my jam!

So, just take a chill pill Sam
I'm about to teach you the game
What we call jive
You call it slang!
We ain't got no to time for squares
Who be acting lame
And on Friday nights
You better be ready to hang!

Cause' it's time to hit the clubs
And hear those groovy cats sang
It feels like magic is in the air
When we're out vibing with the gang
Believe me by 12 o'clock
That joint is in full swang!

Listen old boy, if you ain't heard about Jazz
Then must've been living up in Alcatraz
Yeah, you've missed
A whole lotta "Razzmatazz"
I'm talking about the kind of music
That really works your calves
Cause' it makes you forget your woes
And makes you drop them bags

And just go out and dance
Wearing your finest rags

So, listen Jazz ain't just about playing a gig
It about playing those tunes
That make you flip your wig
Cause' Black folks grind so hard
They really need that jig
So, music became the best part of life
You dig?

Now listen,
Parker and Gillespie use to jam with Monk
And they was some musical genius type Kats
While Miles, Bassie, and Coltrane was smooth
Cause' they knew where vibe was at

And them beboppers
Were really swinging Jack !
I swear they had the dance floor
Under attack!
Cause's that base rhythm was cool
The Brass section was phat
And the hooch was chilling

While them gals was warming up the back
But if you step out of line
You gone catch a real hard slap

Now Louis Armstrong was the man
Yeah, he was a real cool cat
Couldn't nobody touch him
When he started to scat
Be-Bop-a-wa-scittly-dat
Man-O-Man that cat
Knew how to swing that axe
He's the one who really
Put Jazz on the map
Everybody wanted to hear Louis
Lay down those tracks
Drop a dime on the counter
And go spin that wax
Cause' whenever Louis played
The whole joint was packed!

But up at the Cotton Club
Is where Cab Calloway did his thang!
His song "Minnie The Moocher"
Made Black and white folks swang!

But slow down man
Cause' Jazz is part of a Fam
We got all kinds of jams
We got Swing, Bop and Cool Jazz
Now this could get a little tricky
So, pay attention Sam!
Cause' we also have cousins
We called the "Blues"
Yeah, they come from the south
They got some down hearted tunes
And gals like Bessie Smith and Ma Rainey
Knew exactly what to do
Cause' those gals sure had a gift
For mixing Jazz with the Blues
The way they could move a crowd
Them gals could never loose
With those lovesick moods
They knew how to captivate
The gals and the dudes

So, like I said man
Anyone can go to
The Scholl of Jazz
And you don't to be

No college Grad
But you do need to have some chops
And a whole lotta pizzazz
You gotta know how to talk that Jive
And get with the lingo man!
And keep those joints jumping
For those jitterbug fans!

Now listen Daddy-O,
It don't matter if your name is
Lucky Sam
Or
Shy Abraham
All they hear is
Yes, Sir!
Yes Ma'am!
Hot diggity damn
Those cats are playing my jam!

THE HISTORY OF "ROCK AND ROLL"

(It began in the during the late 1940s and early 1950s)

Rock and Roll music is derived from other Black American music styles such as gospel, jump blues, jazz, boogie woogie, rhythm and blues, as well as country music. The origins of rock and roll have been fiercely debated by commentators and historians, however most of them agree that it came from the South.

Later the southern roots of Rock and Roll would be planted in inner-city centers such as St. Louis, Memphis, New York City, Detroit, Chicago, Cleveland, and Buffalo due to the migration of former enslaved African descendants. As a result, black and white residents were now living in close proximity to each other in large numbers and would be able to hear each other's music.

This mix of communities would become transformative as the lyrics in early Rock and Roll songs would focus on issues, events and conflicts that most listeners could relate to through their personal experiences. This new Black music genre was breaking boundaries and expressing emotions that people were actually feeling but had never talked about which resulted in an awakening in younger Americans. Additionally, as radio stations made white and black music available, other music styles such as jazz and swing which were also taken up by white musicians, would contribute to what many called a "cultural collision".

And because of this new networking of Black and White Americans, the music would also have an impact on each other's lifestyles, fashion, attitudes, and language. Indeed, this style of music was crossing over and would inevitably have a profound influence on the civil rights movement, because it changed the way both white and black teenagers identified themselves.

Consequently, the influence of Black music would provoke strong White racist reactions within America, with many Whites condemning its breaking down of barriers based on color. But they would be no match for the power of Rock and Roll and other Black Music genres which had begun leading the way for desegregation, with its strong lyrical content that encouraged racial cooperation by sharing their experiences.

The True Legends Of Rock And Roll

When you think of a Rock Legend
Do you think of someone like Bruce Springsteen
Or Guns and Roses playing for thousands of fans?
When the real truth is that Rock music
Was stolen from Black Musicians
Kind of like the way they stole this
Native American land

It's been said that Rock and Roll was born in the 50's
During the civil rights movement
When Black folks didn't receive a lot of good will
A time when most of them were just poor folks
Trying to earn a decent living
Just so they could pay their bills

But the more those Black artists tried to grow
The more their music was marginalized
And the more White teenagers wanted to hear it
The more some white folks wanted to see our demise
Cause' when it came to Black music
The older White folks just wanted to criticize

White churches used to call it Satan's music
And they said it needed to be sanitized
They said Black music should be banned
Because it was becoming a threat to their lives

They used to say that our music was lower class
Therefore, it shouldn't be recognized
Yet our music would become revolutionary
To their dismay and fearsome surprise
Because White teenagers would eventually rebel
Against their elder's bigotry and lies

So, White record labels crafted a plan
To try and stop the African descendants rise
They used a White singer named Elvis
To steal our black music
So, they could grow their
White's only enterprise

In actuality it was a Black artist
Named Big Mama Thornton
Who recorded the song "Hound Dog" first!
Yet White folks recorded it with Elvis
And threw Big Mamma's version under the dirt!

But then there was another Black song called
"Johnny B Good"
And those teens were completely in awe of it
Even though the music came from
A Black artist named Chuck Berry
Those White teens still wanted to hear all of it!

Then there was a Black artist named Little Richard
Who made all the fans scream his name
When he performed the hit song "Long Tall Sally"
Their reactions were always the same

And Fats Domino was another powerhouse
Who had some great sounds too
He said his smash hit song "I'm Walking"
Was really just a variation of Rhythm and Blues
He told folks that he'd been playing that music
Down in New Orleans
And, for him Rock and Roll wasn't nothing new

Later on, the radio stations began see the potential
Of the Black musicians path to fortune and fame
So, they began to play Black Music on the air
Because the demand from White teenagers

Could no longer be contained
And it became overwhelmingly obvious to everyone
That the music world was about to change

You must understand that
Rock and Roll didn't simply emerge
It was a force that came charging through the air
With the energy of a supersonic bang
That was creating ripple effects everywhere

Listen, the way Rock and Roll was combined
The musical possibilities simply boggled the mind
Cause' it was a blend of R&B, Pop and Country
That was unlike any other style at that time

And the vocals were rich, raw and robust
With a tone that was grungy and rasping
The guitar sounds like it almost has a growl
And the beat of those drums
Just kept on tapping

It was more than a new music genre
It grew into a distinct musical class
Cause' Black folks didn't just create new music

They created a legacy that was made to last

They miraculously made something beautiful
In spite of the ugliness of Jim Crow and segregation
And Black voices were starting to be heard
Through a means of mass media communication

Rock and Roll music was so relatable
That it helped Black and White kids
Find some common ground
And for Black Musicians that was a blessing
Cause' no one could ever replace
That authentic Rock and Roll sound

So, the next time you think of a Rock Legend
Don't just think of someone like Bruce Springsteen
Or Guns and Roses playing for thousands of fans
Think about how Rock music was stolen
From Black Musicians
Kind of like the way they stole this
Native American land

THE HISTORY OF THE AFRO-LATINO INFUSION
(1500's – 1600's)

During the 15th and 16th centuries, West Africans were brought to Latin America through the Atlantic slave trade, to be used as agricultural, domestic, menial laborers and mineworkers. The Caribbean's and South America would receive 95 percent of the Africans with only 5 percent going to Northern America. This added population of Africans would lead to a blending of cultures which would create new and unique forms of Language, Religions, Music, Martial Arts and Dance.

But, as we focus on the music History, we can see that African culture had a profound influence on Latin American music because it introduced Latins to new rhythms, drumming with traditional beats and unique sounds that were part of African culture. A lot of experts believe that this African influence was the biggest factor in the evolution of Latin American tunes as we know them today. If you look at styles like Salsa and Samba, as well as Merengue you will most definitely notice the

African influence that is now a distinct feature in Latin American music.

It is said that music was man's most powerful creation because it is the one language that everybody can understand. While it's certainly true that music has progressed over time, it's still worth knowing the history behind it all. Sometimes it's hard to say what makes music so special, but we do know that it can bring people together and force them to set aside their differences.

Yet, in many of those Latin American countries, Black Hispanics would encounter similar issues of discrimination as Black Americans had also encountered in the US. It has been said that Latin countries such as Cuba, Mexico, Puerto Rico, Brazil, Honduras, Argentina, Dominican Republic have long histories of discrimination against our darker skinned brethren within their own population even to this day.

The Afro-Latino Infusion

Hello, my Latino Brothers and Sisters
(Hola mis hermanos y hermanas espanoles)
I came here to dispel any disillusions
Africans and Hispanics have much in common
Please allow me to clear up any confusion
African Slaves also landed in South America
And our ancestors created an Afro-Latino infusion

We know that Afro-Latino's share our African Roots
Although some might try to hide it
The same music infusion that occurred in the U.S.
Occurred in Latin America, and no one can deny it

Africans had a great impact on Latin Music
Yes, that common heritage lives inside us
You can hear the influences in Cuba and Puerto Rico
We are African descendants, so let no man divide us

Our Ancestors would meet and mingle at seaports
Exchanging different dances, songs and rhythms
Creating musical genres that were distinctly unique
That's how we came into this multi-cultural position

Yes, the Spanish and Portuguese had their own music
But let it be known my sisters and brothers
That Hispanic music was also influenced by Africans
Who created Samba, Salsa, Rumba
And many others

Family we may not speak the same language
But we do share the language of music
And it's not about the hand your given
It's about how you decide to use it

We come from different paths
But on this journey, we are together
Remember there's power in numbers
So, let us learn to lean on each other

Black American music has genres like
Like Blues, Jazz, Hip-Hop and R&B
But your Mambo, Tango and Reggaeton
Sure, sounds good to me!

So, the next time you play that Reggaeton beat
Be proud that it comes from an African descent
For there's so much richness in our heritage

It's more than a flag that we represent

There should be no prejudices among us
No matter if we are Spanish or born in the U.S.
The African bloodline is within us
And unity is what we should profess

So, remember my Brothers and Sisters
(Hola mis hermanos y hermanas espanoles)
That today I came here to dispel any disillusions
For Africans and Hispanics have much in common
I hope I was able to clear up any confusion
Yes, African Slaves landed in South America
And our ancestors created an Afro-Latino infusion

We know that Afro-Latino's share our African Roots
Although some might try to hide it
Cause' the same music infusion
That occurred in the U.S.
Occurred in Latin America
And no one can deny it

THE HISTORY OF CIVIL RIGHTS
(1950's – 1960's)

Most Americans today have probably read something about the Civil Rights movement and some of the monumental events that occurred back then. But what if you were to pause for a moment and imagine that you lived back in those hard times when freedom was just a dream, and you've made the choice as a Black musician to become a part of history by using your voice to empower the Black Civil Rights movement. Because back then folks didn't do it for the money or the fame, they did it for the benefit of Black people. I believe that if you could walk in their shoes for an instant, you would undoubtedly have much more appreciation for those artist and the musicians who led us by their examples and not just their words during those repressive times.

Fortunately, African descendants now live in a time where Black artists have the freedom to create music without the fear of dire repercussions or consequences because we have now been granted the right to free speech which was part of those Civil Rights that our ancestors bled and died for. And because of their bravery and courage to stand up, we are now able to freely speak out through our music without serious retribution. So, as you read some of the history in this book maybe you can also take a moment as I did and look back upon our ancestors to see the road that was paved for us. I hope that you will also take great pride in knowing that it was their contributions that helped America transition into a new era of social tolerance and inclusion.

1955: Rosa Parks and the Montgomery Bus Boycott
1957: The Little Rock Nine and the Little Rock Central High School Integration
1960: The Greensboro Four and the Sit-In Movement
1960: Ruby Bridges and the New Orleans School Integration
1961: Freedom Rides
1963: Birmingham Demonstrations
1963: March on Washington
1964: Civil Rights Act
1964: Fannie Lou Hamer's Testimony at the Democratic Convention
1965: Assassination of Malcolm X
1965: Selma-Montgomery March
1965: Watts Riots
1966: Black Panther Party founded
1967: Loving v. Virginia
1967: Detroit Riot
1968: Assassination of Martin Luther King, Jr.

Music Of The Movement

I hope this poem provides you
With new insights and revelations
About the songs that helped to inspire
The Civil Right movement generation
Because there is no doubt
That it was truly a masterful combination
When Black leadership and Black Musicians
Came together for a worthy collaboration
So today, I honor them
With my respect and appreciation
For having the courage to stand up
For the survival of the Black population!

Listen, that was the era
That laid the foundation
For Black voter Rights
And cancelling discrimination
Leaving behind Jim Crow
And the era of Segregation
As Black folks were bravely protesting
And singing songs about Black liberation!

We had endured way too many tragedy's
And it was time for us to stand up
Cause' Black folks in America
Truly had enough!
They told America that
There would be no more sitting
In the back of the bus for us!
As a result, sometimes they were killed
Or beaten and taken away in handcuffs

And with every cruel gesture
They wrote songs about the oppressor
Black folks were so united
That America began to feel the pressure

While Black Musicians were taking notes
Writing powerful songs
That would inspire us with hope
Cause' like Fannie Lou Hammer said
All citizens deserve the right to vote!

So, when The Impressions sang
"People Get Ready"
Their hearts were truly with it

And when James Brown sang
"I'm Black and I'm Proud"
That message was definitely transmitted!
Because with every line and every verse
It was our people who benefited
Those songs became the glue
That kept our ancestors committed

Cause' the music of that generation
Was about promoting solidarity
To support our liberation
And those songs hit differently
When they included those daily affirmations
Cause' songs like "Message From A Blackman"
Kept them fortified with self-love and determination

So, when we "Lift Every Voice and Sing"
We can hear the dream of Dr. King
Telling those racists politicians
That it's time to "Let Freedom Ring"

I bet it seemed like every hour
Somebody was playing
The Isley Brothers "Fight The Power"

And I can imagine that
When the days were dark and long
Somebody was playing Marvin Gaye's
"What's Going On"
Once again Black folks created a new genre
Now we call them freedom Songs

So, when Sam Cooke sang
"A Change Is Gonna Come"
The lyrics became our creed
Just hearing his smooth vocals
Let us know that eventually
We would succeed
Cause' the music had a purpose
And that was to plant the seeds

Even when we suffered through retaliation
And we saw our beloved leader's bleed
It was Dr. King who told them
"You can kill the dreamer
But you can't kill the dream"

Cause' the movement was about the future
Of Black descendants

They wanted us to have collective wealth too
They didn't want to see us dependent

But White folks were saying
That it was the constitution they were defending
While Black folks said if that's the truth
Then America needs to stop pretending
Cause' it appears that our hopes and dreams
Are constantly pending
And how can you say we're all Americans
When it's Black lives that keep descending
You're keeping us poor with your practices
Like unfair bank loans and underhanded lending

Cause' White folk were making progress
While they were also nickel and diming
So, Black folks needed protection
From that district redlining
And all that racial profiling

Listen, that was the generation that finally stood up
To address the people's fears and questions
So those songs will always represent
The Civil Rights Movement selection

And that music should be a part of
Every American's collection!
So that we'll be able to recall those voices
That took America in a new direction

That's why I look up to our kin folks
Who despite having the doors slammed in their face
They still found the strength
To fight this country's prejudice and the hate

So, I'm grateful to Dr. King
Who wanted to peacefully conversate
Although tragically he was killed
By their fear, violence and hate

And I'm thankful for brother Malcom
Who had the mind to see
That although they called us Americans
We still weren't free

And I respect Nina Simone who once said
"It's an artist's duty to reflect the times"
So, she wrote songs that were so powerful
That Black and White Folks had to fall in line

Let me hear you say power to the Queen!
And raise your fist one time!

But, I hope this poem has given you
Some new insights and revelations
About the songs that helped to inspire
The Civil Right movement generation
Because there is no doubt
That it was truly a masterful combination
When Black leadership and Black Musicians
Came together for an unbreakable collaboration
That's why I chose to I honor them
With my respect and appreciation
For having the courage to stand up
For the survival of Black, the population!

THE LEGENDARY NINA SIMONE
(February 21, 1933 – April 21, 2003)

Nina Simone's was an Artist who believed that being Black in America meant that we are often times forced to deal with things that are difficult to realize. She also knew that fear would drive many Black people into a subdued existence. But she didn't want to take the easy road, instead Nina wanted retaliation through her music. Nina's music was unbound by any standards or rules. She made many musical contributions to the civil rights movement, that were laced with confrontational choruses. Her Black power stance was in every note, every forceful breath and pause—because not only was she saying what others wouldn't, but she was saying it using profanity at a time that was unheard of. She was cursing out those still enforcing Jim Crow, and to an America that was betraying its own people. Dick Gregory commented on one of her songs, stating that, "not one black man would dare say 'Mississippi Goddam'."

Her famous friend, author James Baldwin, said that "it's crucial to the Black experience to have our existence reflected by Black artists, to reinforce our humanity, to communicate and insist on our personhood beyond our own communities. Black music provides an anchor in and of itself for us."

Boldly, Nina Simone expressed a solemn duty to Black people, and the impact it had on her career was evident yet that was decades ago. Consequently, in these current times where things are supposed to be significantly more equal, one might be hard pressed to find performers as bold as she was throughout her life. Nina will always be our High Priestess of Soul who continues to inspires us with her music.

The Power Of Nina's Blues

Today, let us raise one fist for Nina Simone

Because she was so much more than

A musical prodigy

Yes, she was classically trained

But she was still seen as an oddity

Cause' Nina knew that being born black in America

Shouldn't have to come with no apology

And that her genius was far too great

For her gifts to be given modestly!

Her talent was undeniable

Her magnificence

Needed no concessions

Cause' she was a mind liberator

Through musical expression

She made awakening minds

Her primary profession

And that's why Nina always be

One of our greatest Black Legends!

Some say she was a riddle of complexities

Some say that she was an anomaly

Because her strength and her brilliance

Was a reflection of African genealogy
And she had a voice that was
So powerful and dynamic
That she must have been a prophecy!

Nina was "Young Gifted and Black"
So, naturally she spoke out against
The atrocities and social confrontations
And about hate crimes like
Church bombings and lynching's
As well as the inequality of segregation
Yes, she blessed us with
Ballads and songs
That will surely last for generations
Cause's her messages were on point
And her lyrics were bold and earth shaking

Nina was truly ahead of her time
She was our "High Priestess of Soul"
And one of our greatest Black minds
That's why during those dark
And tragic times
We needed to have artist like Nina Simone
Standing on the front line!

Nina wanted to see us "Feeling Good"
Not all depressed and sad
So, she sat down at that keys
And played "Mr. Backlash"
And when they killed those 4 little girls
Nina was just as outraged and mad
So, she sat down once again
And played "Mississippi Goddam"

Her songs were powerful and audacious
Because they were a reflection of Black life
And Nina didn't worry about no retribution
Instead, she wanted us to fight

She was a proud supporter of the movement
When Black streets were stained with red
She was a of beacon of hope for our people
At a time when so many of our leaders bled
But she never hesitated to stand up
And say what needed to be said
Because true lioness follows her heart
And doesn't let fears control her head

No, it wasn't easy speaking out
Some folks paid a heavy price
But Nina just kept on singing
About our pain and strife

Her commitment was steadfast
And she always had a hand to lend
She was supported civil rights leaders
And celebrated poets
So, they blessed her pen
Nina called Langston Hughes
And James Baldwin
Two of her closest friends

But when the media tried to question her
Nina didn't hesitate to push back
She said you see I have no other choice
Cause' it's such a beautiful thing to be Black

She sparked needed conversations
But kept her people inspired
She devoted her life to fighting oppression
And that's why Nina was so admired

She never turned a blind eye
She was a part of the solution
She didn't stand on the sidelines
She was a soldier of the revolution

Nina was tenacious and unapologetic
Because Black liberation is what she seeked
Let us give thanks to the Black Goddess
Cause' her beauty was beyond skin deep
And she never wanted to fit in
Because she was a true Black sheep
But she left footprints that were so deep
That they had to bronze her feet!

So, let's raise one fist for Nina Simone
Because she was so much more than
A musical prodigy
Yes, she was classically trained
But she was still seen as an oddity
Cause' Nina knew that being born black in America
Shouldn't have to come with no apology
And that her genius was far too great
For her gifts to be given modestly!

Her talent was undeniable

Her magnificence

Needed no concessions

Cause' she was a mind liberator

Through musical expression

She made awakening minds

Her primary profession

And that's why Nina always be

One of our greatest Black Legends!

THE HISTORY OF R&B
(Early To Mid-1950s)

Rhythm and Blues, also known as *R&B*, is a genre of popular music that originated in the Black American community during the 1940s. Initially, R&B songs were commonly written about Black folks experiences with pain and suffering, our quest for freedom, our longing for comfort and happiness, topics about our triumphs and failures in relationships, our dissatisfaction with economics situations, and some of our deepest desires for love. This is why many R&B listeners tend to strongly identify with its audacious and alluring lyrics. Yet, in the early 1940's this genre was only appreciated by Black Americans who were the only consumers of Black music. This minimal number of sales was happening because at that time there was no white radio air play happening for Black music. However, during the early 1950s, more White teenagers would become aware of R&B and other Black music genres, and they would begin to purchase Black music. Thus, as the awareness of Black music began to grow, White teens across the country would undoubtedly become true fans of Black music.

Essentially, when we make music about true life experiences it becomes relevant to our daily lives thereby converting millions of listeners into loyal fans. Indeed, music is a powerful force because it's capable of speaking to our hidden desires and its listeners can devour the lyrics like food for the soul. And R&B is that kind of music that gives listeners a release from their heart ache and pain by granting them a small reprieve from their day to day stresses. Just by playing the right tune, the mind can be transported to a soothing place of wonder and happiness. Hence, R&B can reach into your heart and hold you so close that you'll never wanna let go of that feeling. This music is perfect for those winter nights when you find yourself tossing and turning and you need a something to rock you to sleep. So, it's my pleasure to introduce the irreplaceable sounds of R&B.

For The Love Of R&B

Good evening and thank you
For listening to R&B
And "If This World Was Mine"
I'd only give you the kind of music
That would make your soul unwind
I'd be waiting for you at home
It will be "Always and Forever"
Just "You And I"
I swear I'll put a smile on your face every time
And even set the mood while you dine
Oh, "If This World Was Mine"
Life would be so sublime!
The things that I would do
"If This World Were Mine"

Darlin, if this world was mine!
And you needed an emotional break
I'd bless you with Erykah Badu's serenades
And ignite you with the soul of Mary J
I'd have Janet take you out on an "Escapade"
You know that R&B will always be there
To ease your pain

They say that true love last
For more than a season
And if love doesn't last
I've heard all of the "Reasons"
So, just listen to R&B
And "Don't Say Goodnight"
Cause' if you give me the "Green light"
I promise that my "Red Light Special"
Will bring you "Back To Life"
I'll make your soul take flight
Cause' you can always count on me
To get you through the night

Oh Darlin, if this world was mine!
I would only bring you gratification
I'll comfort you with
The O'Jays
The Whispers
The Manhattans
And The Temptations
Then I'll smooth it out
With "It's Just My Imagination"

And I can tell that "Lately"

You've been feeling Idle
Baby, if this world was mine
Every night would be an R&B revival
Believe me music is definitely the key
To your spiritual survival
R&B can take you higher
Then Miriah's highest note
"If Only For One Night"
Let's "Rock The Boat"
I can "Make It Last Forever"
So, you'll never be alone

You know that "I Will Always Love You"
And I'll always "Give You Something That You Can Feel"
You can always count on me darlin
Cause' "Baby I'm For Real"
And my "Whip Appeal"
"Has Got To Be Real"

You can listen to R&B
When your soul needs some satisfaction
And I'll bless you with some
Luther Vandross and Freddy Jackson

I'll make life much sweeter
And I'll never leave you "Weak"
I'll just let the sounds of Stevie
"Knock you Off your Feet"

And you know "I'll Be There"
When life has you reeling
And baby when you get that feeling
I'll hit you with Marvin's "Sexual Healing"

Or when you're feeling a little sad and blue
I'll play Patti LaBelle's "If You Only Knew"
Cause' R&B has your back
Babe, it's all about you!

I know sometimes it's "Hard To Say Good-Bye"
And bad breakups can leave you in distress
So, I'll feed your soul with Otis Redding's
"Try A Little Tenderness"

And when it really gets rough
And life seems so cruel
Cause old lovers say
"I want you back"

Just to leave you feeling confused
Don't let those heartless words
Play with your mind!
Instead, I want you to dry your "Ebony Eyes"
And tell them you've had "One Last Cry"
So "What's Love Got To Do With It"
"Let's Just Kiss And Say Goodbye"
Oh, my darlin the things I'd do for you
"If This World Were Mine"!

Good evening, R&B!
And thank you for all of the love, that you've given me!
You've always been so compassionate and kind
You fill me with so much hope
It's almost like you can read my mind
Because of you I know "The Power of Love"
So, believe me if there is a next time
I mean "If Ever I Fall In Love"
It won't be "No Ordinary Love"
Cause' I wanna be "Crazy In Love"
I wanna be "Drunk In Love"
"Till The Cops Come Knocking" kind of Love
Yes, I want that "Endless Love"
Not some half time love

Or "Rude Boy" kind of love
Cause' now "I Have A Vision Of Love"
And they are not
"All I Need To Get By"
So, I'll tell them I'm not
"Living For The Love Of You"
And I remember when you was my Boo
But now I'm no longer caught up in
"The Sweetest Taboo"
So, I will survive
And you're just a liar
Trying to kill my vibe
With that "Fire and Desire"
So, R&B come hit me
With that Earth, Wind and Fire

Cause' "I've heard it all before"
No, you can't have my peace
And believe me that music hit different
When I was going through grief

But " I found love on a two way street"
And I realized that it was only me
Who was giving

But now thanks to R&B
I'm getting back to living
Yes "I found Love Under New Management"
And my "Love Hangover" is finally gone
Because I fell in love with R&B
During "The Quiet Storm"
With no interruptions
Or commercial breaks
And now I know in my heart
That I'm in a good place!

So, I've dried my "Ebony Eyes"
And I've had that "One Last Cry"
So, "What's Love Got To Do With It"
"Let's Just Kiss And Say Goodbye"
Oh, "If This World Was Mine"
Life would be so sublime!
The things that I would do
"If This World Were Mine"

THE HISTORY OF HIP HOP
(The Bronx, New York 1970's)

You could say that the Blues is the great, great Grandparent of *Hip Hop* music which was conceived in the early 1970s up in the *Boggie Down* Bronx, New York. This was back in the day when Black communities would host block parties where DJ's or Disk Jockey's would play the percussion breaks of popular songs using two turntables and a mixer so they could seamlessly blend the percussion breaks from two copies of the same record. The DJ would accomplish this by playing both records simultaneously and then alternating between each turntable to create a continuous extension of the percussionist *break*. But, that continuous rhythm also became the perfect base for the *Rap Artist* who made an art out of *"Spitten Bars"* or talking over the beat. This style of music would become another variation of the Blues that was conceived by innovative Black minds who would produce an alternative music genre that would emerge from the streets of New York City.

However, because those DJ's were sampling beats from another Artist works, it was not yet considered to be a viable art. But the potential was already there, so they went from the streets to the studio where they could create their own beats. And that was the moment when Hip Hop was officially born, but it all started with *DJ Kool Herc* who had *One Mic*, two turntables, record crates and the ingenuity to lay down the foundation for a new culture of Rappers, Break Dancers, Graffiti Artist and some Human Beatboxers which is an artist who can make beat sounds from their mouth.

Later, the world would realize that Hip Hop was not like any other musical genre, because it was also seen as new culture for the youth. Hip Hop would later catapult many young Black artist to a level of success that they never could have imagined, and with their popularity and status some would also become movie stars as well. Hence, the world would once again witness the power of our African heritage and our ability to influence American music culture.

NYC Mic Checker

Let me tell you how I grew up
In the Hip Hop Mecca
The original microphone checker
Yeah, NYC is the home of trend setters
And the birth of Hip Hop go getters
Like
Tupac
KRS One
And everybody
Knew P-Diddy
Plus, we had
Mary J. Blige
Method Man
Rakim
And that "Bad Boy" Biggie!

Listen, Hip Hop was founded by D.J. Kool Herc
And emcees who spit barz like "La Di Da Di"
It started with some kids just looking for fun
We wasn't trying to change the music world
It was a side hustle and a hobby

But then Kool Herc did something amazing

He started improvising at block parties
Man, we loved how he mixed those records
While we sipped on that cola and Bacardi

Herc started spinning records
Up in the Bronx around 1973
Back then I think everybody
Was trying to be an Emcee
He would pull up in a van
With turn tables and record crates
And used the electricity from a light pole
Just by unscrewing the base

We all studied his techniques
And waited for the rhythm to break
While other kids would just record it
So, they could sell some mix-tapes

And the crowds started getting so big
It was like having a concert in our backyards
We even had the 5% Nation come through
Shouting peace, to the Earths and the Gods
And to the old folks who set up the tables
So, they could play a few games of dominos and cards

Cause' those block parties were the best
When we use to dance in the park
Rocking the latest fly gear
Waiting for some convo to spark

Back in the day the vibe was lit!
And those fish fry dinners were amazing
I remember how the base was bumping
And the speakers were always blazing

Back then I was a young fly girl
With the baby hair and the big gold hoops
And the Brothas would be tryna holla
When me and my crew came by the stoop

Cause' we always kept it 100
We wasn't all fake and phony
And when we stepped up in the party
We rolled with some cool ass homies

We knew that we had a bond
And that was our love for Hip Hop
That means we would jam together
Whether we were good friends or not

So, it didn't matter
If we were from Brooklyn or the Bronx
Or if we wore the color blue or red
It didn't matter
What neighborhood we were from
As long as our souls were being fed
We were "One Nation Under A Groove"
Rocking to the beats in our heads

That's why Hip Hop was so healing
Cause' the music gave us life
And if it wasn't for our music
We wouldn't have
Soul Train in the morning
Or the Apollo Theater at night
And we wouldn't set the trends
That keeps our gear looking tight

Listen, Hip Hop represented Black American culture
And it gave our young minds a sense of peace
Cause' as good as the party ended that night
We couldn't wait to do it again next week!

So, this is what it was like for me growing up

In the Hip Hop Mecca

The original microphone checker

Yeah, NYC is the home of trend setters

And the birth of Hip Hop go getters

Like

Tupac

KRS One

And everybody

Knew P-Diddy

Plus, we had

Mary J. Blige

Method Man

Rakim

And that "Bad Boy" Biggie!

Why I Love Hip Hop

I'll tell you why I love Hip-Hop
Cause' back in the day
When I lived on the block
I remember when DJ Kool Herc
And DJ Grand Master Flash
Used to buy albums from the record shops
And I still remember when
Biz Markie and Doug E. Fresh
Started the human beat box!

Listen, R.A.P. stands for
Rhythm-And-Poetry
So, no we don't do it for play
And we don't do it for kicks
And the truth be told
We're real sensitive about our shit!

So, Hip Hop was never a vice
Cause' it helped me get through
The B.S. in life
Listen, sometimes we would disagree
And sometimes we would even fight

But none of us would ever bite
Cause' stealing another Emcees rhymes
Is considered to be impolite!

But we came from an era
That use to shoot the dozens
That means we'll rap about
Yo mama, yo daddy, yo aunt
And yo cousin

But the lethal one's spit verses
Like lyrical assassins
So, you better run for cover
Cause' they're coming out blasting
And the weak ones
Yawl get eaten for breakfast
Like they just finished fasting

Cause' if you step to the wrong one
Then you might get smoked
That's why everybody knew
That Rakim wasn't no joke

So, if you ain't ready

You need to bone up
Yo, perfect your craft!
Time to hone up!
Cause' real emcee's
Rhyme with fatal intentions
Just like Lauryn Hill crushed the competition
In every dimension

Artist like K.R.S. just did it with audacity
And Big Daddy-Kane did it with tenacity
Eminem was able to freestyle at a higher capacity
But 2-Pac just did it naturally

And Snoop Dog had crazy Bars
But I think skills were underrated
And Dr. Dre's beats were off the hook
Cause' that "G Thang" track was totally elevated
The whole collaboration was on point
And their talents were demonstrated
Listen, that's the type of work
That deserves to be Grammy nominated

But the Wu-Tang Clan came out the gate
Like soldiers running drills

I mean the whole crew was nice
I'm just saying for real!

No doubt Method Man's had the best verses
Yo, the Brotha had mad skills!
But I dig the way they supported each other
So, they could all pay their mamma's bills

But I remember when RAP was underground
When artists like Kool-Moe-Dee and Rob Base
Was chilling at the clubs
Up in the Boogie Down
Cause' the Bronx was popping
And fans were coming from miles around

But on Friday night
It's time to break your stash
If you wanted to see
DJ Afrika Bambaataa
Battle DJ Grand Master Flash

Yeah, Hip Hop was doing great
And everybody played mix tapes
So, it didn't matter if you

Lived in the suburbs
Or you lived on Section-8
Cause' rap music was so dope
That it even made White teens wanna relate

It was beautiful seeing Hip Hop starting to rise
As rappers' names were being emphasized
P-Diddy started taking calls
To grow his Bad Boy enterprise
While Biggie Smalls was going
From New York to worldwide
M-TV Hip Hop Awards were being televised
Cause' a powerful music genre
Was being recognized

Listen Artist started becoming producers
And some producers became exect's
Cause' the R.A.P. game
Was finally getting the proper respect

But let's take a moment
To speak on the Queens
Who fearlessly rocked the mic
Yeah, I'm talking about

Queen Latifah
Monie-Love
And Emcee Lyte
Plus, we had
Salt and Pepper
Roxanne
And Lisa Left Eye
We had Da-Bratt
And Foxy Brown
With Missy's Supa Dupa Fly

Yeah, I remember the first time
That I heard Remy Ma spit
Between her Foxy and Lil-Kim
It was hard for me to pick

But they paved the way for artists
Like Niki, Megan and Cardi-B
Who took the female rap game
To a whole other degree!

Listen, Hip Hop literally
Started in the streets
Where DJ's were

Sampling all kinds of beats
They sampled the Blues
Jazz, Rock and Pop
It really didn't matter
As long as they could
Make the beat drop

And now Rapping was considered
To be a serious art
Because of artist like the Sugar Hill Gang
And Run-D-Mc
Who were blowing up on the record charts

Then we had Hip Hop Junkies
Like Nice and Smooth
And Will Smith and Jazzy Jeff
Came out with that "Summer Time" tune

Plus, we all knew he was gonna be a star
When we saw LL Cool-Jay making moves
Right after they shot that Hip Hop movie
Called "Crush Groove"

Listen Hip Hop was turning into a beast

And everybody was getting bigger
Jay-z became Jigga
And Busta was checking for Ra-Digger
While Kanye was spitting bars
About them "Gold Diggers"

Cause' for Black folks
Music ain't just lyrical
It's about real life
It's about how we live
So, yeah sometimes it's gets political
That's why we needed artists
Like Jill Scott and Erykah Badu
Working with "The Roots"
And others like
Public Enemy
"Nas" and "Common"
Who could spit dat truth
Yeah, they were planting the seeds
So, that we could harvest the fruit

And because of artist like
Busta Rhymes
DMX

Rakim and Jay-Z
Rap was able to transcend languages
And take Hip Hop music overseas

Listen Hip Hop is a culture
So, you gotta spit it with emotion!
And every great Emcee knows
How each verse needs to be spoken!

Because their fans learn the songs
And verses become etched in their brains
That's how a lot of the creatives
Are really getting paid
Cause' now they got merchandise
Branded with the artists name!

Listen, the language of music is powerful
It can go from a poem into a song
And verses can go into a ballad
That can express all of our rights
And our wrongs

Cause' the poem is the lyrics
And hook can sound like a chant

But an oldie but and goodie
Still makes old folks wanna dance

And what a boring world it would be
Without the phenomenal Hip Hop sound
So, thanks to all of the artists and musicians
Who did our people proud!

And that's why I'll always love Hip-Hop!
Cause' Back in the day
When I lived on the block
I remember when DJ Kool Herc
And DJ Grand Master Flash
Used to buy albums from the record shops
And I still remember when
Biz Markie and Doug E. Fresh
Started the human beat box!

Listen, R.A.P. stands for
Rhythm-And-Poetry
So, no we don't do it for play
And we don't do it for kicks
And the truth be told
We're real sensitive about our shit!

THE HISTORY OF BLACK MUSIC CREATORS
(The first African landing occurred in late August of 1619)

Africans and their descendants have been fighting to gain total equality since the first Africans were brought to America in 1619. In spite of our perseverance, we are still finding that even today the recording industries in the United States have been routinely underpaying Black American artists. These misdeeds have long been suspected by performers, their families, music fans, scholars and critics. We only need to look at the negligent and even fraudulent accounting practices that have blatantly denied Black American artists and their families opportunities to accumulate wealth and achieve seemingly middle class status which is what the American dream is supposed to be about.

"Systematic exploitation and appropriation of Black American music reflects patterns of relationships established during and after slavery. Slave plantations were business enterprises that accounted for their most valuable assets — slaves — in ways that continue to shape business practice today."

It can be said that Black-American musical forms did have a positive effect on African descendants and their communities, however they still have only been offered slivers of opportunities for wealth in comparison to their White counterparts. Many Black Americans turned to musical entertainment because there were limited socially sanctioned avenues of employment for Black Americans during and after slavery. Yet, why are we still seeing well into the 20th century a continuation of pervasive formal and informal modes of social control. Indeed, we have come a long way, but it is just as much evident that we still have further to go.

It is my belief that recalling our History is important for the purpose of establishing a benchmark for how successful we merely think we are. Given that fact, I've come to the conclusion that it is probable that racism has been around so long that it's become as American as apple pie. Racism never truly went away; it just became subtle like the stiches that seem to blend into the American Flag. You know that the stitch work is there, but it's not supposed to be seen, it's supposed to go unnoticed and give off the illusion of something that has been well made. The problem with that theory is that once you can see the flaws those stiches, they become overwhelmingly obvious to even the blindest of eyes.

That being said, at the very least I hope that you have also begun to notice the patterns of injustice and inequality that have been hidden before you in plain sight. I also hope that I have exposed some of those hanging threads and intricate flaws within the patch work of the American society that we all share.

The Black Creatives

It's no coincidence that Black creatives
Aren't more recognized
For our artistic creations, innovations
Or world music domination
So, it's understandable if we feel some aggravation
Or become offended when we get
Passed over for their award nominations
Since we know that it was Black music
That laid the foundation
Of course, it's nice to receive applause
And admiration
But many of us still die poor
Due to a lack of compensation

And we already know that our music deserves
Praise and appreciation
Yet some might try to criticize us so they can
Reduce our profits with condemnation

However, when it starts to become popular
They try to steal our creations
By calling it musical integration

Or some type of assimilation
Oh, but today I think they call it
Cultural appropriation
Which is really just more exploitation
Of an already marginalized population!

So, as a Black creative
We can't just rise to rise
We have to rise so that we can open up
Narrow hearts and minds

So, let's get it done
No, we ain't got time to lose
Cause' folks who ain't even been born yet
Are already counting on you!

We definitely got work to do
And continuing this legacy
Is going to take all of you
Listen, this is about helping
The next generation make it through
And that's why we were born
With the talent to breakthrough
So, go ahead and do what you do

Tell them about the history of your Blues
Then give them testimonies
Like only we can do!
No, we don't walk on water
Nor can we turn water into wine
Yet Black creatives are miracles of the divine
Cause' we can turn work songs into Gospel
When we began to improvise
And turn Gospel into the Blues and Jazz
Our talents simply boggle the mind

But don't get too upset
Because we are more than blessed
Even though the life of a Black Creative
Sometimes feels like a test
And many times, our lives
Are filled with strife and stress
But remember we won't live with regrets
Cause' we refuse to digress
Instead, we meditate and rest
So, we can go out and manifest!

And no, we're not always wealthy and famous
But we are definitely rich

Cause' we were handpicked by God
For our special gifts

Yeah, we were made for this
They should throw us a parade for this
Cause' our Ancestors paved the way for this
They dedicated their lives and prayed for this!
Some gave their blood, sweat and tears
So, without a doubt we deserve to get paid for his

And the path for Black creatives
Isn't always golden
Yet here we stand as the elites
Because we are the chosen
So, to our history and culture
We must remain beholden

However, just because we're selected
Doesn't mean that we are always protected
In fact, many times we're disrespected
So, it's reasonable to feel a little neglected

But, please have no fear
Because there's so much power

In the way we execute it
That's why sometimes we're hated
Or end up being persecuted
Yet our genius is too extraordinary
For it to be vague or convoluted
Because our God given talents
Are so deeply rooted

So, the History of Black Music
Must be properly vetted
Because today, many seem to forget it
Which is why we receive less credit
And far too many debits
But they won't know our History
Unless we take control and spread it

Listen,
Louis Armstrong
B.B. King
Chuck Berry
You know they did that
Michael Jackson
Prince
And

Aretha
They blew a hole in Ya cap
And if that wasn't enough
We flipped it and gave you more genres
Like Afro-Latino, Neo Soul, Reggae and Rap

So, the next time they talk about Black creatives
Make sure you tell them
To put some respek on our name
Cause' we don't just create the arts
We change the game
They gave us lemons
But we took it and made lemonade
Out of our suffering and pain
Believe me if it wasn't for the genius of Africans
World music wouldn't even sound the same

So, it's no coincidence that they don't recognize us
For our artistic creations, innovations
Or world music domination
And it's understandable for us
To feel some aggravation
Or become offended when we get
Passed over for their award nominations

Since we know that it was Black music
That laid the foundation
Of course, it's nice to receive applause
And admiration
But many of us still die poor
Due to a lack of compensation

And we already know that our music deserves
Praise and appreciation
Yet some might try to criticize us so they can
Reduce our profits with condemnation

However, when it starts to become popular
They wanna try and steal our creations
By calling it musical integration
Or some type of assimilation
Oh, but today I think they call it
Cultural appropriation
Which is really just more exploitation
Of an already marginalized population!

Thank You For Reading
"Tracing Black Music To The Roots"

By: Sharran C. Taylor

A.K.A. Poet Kween Yakini

Ways That You Can Support An Artist:

Most artists do what they do because they have a love and strong desire for creativity, and any amount of kindness that you can show them is always appreciated. For them this maybe their life's work, and your support would mean than you know. That being said, here are few a ways to show support to an author or any type of artist at very little cost to you.

Support them by following them on social media and share their work and tag the artist in that post

Support them by recommending their works to co-workers, friends or family

Show them support by giving them a positive review to encourage other viewers to purchase a copy their work

Support them by attending some of their events

Show support by telling them how much enjoy their work and what their work has meant to you personally

Offer them a featured showing or performance and/or schedule them as an interview guest on your platform

Also you can show support by making any size donation that you feel comfortable with or by purchasing a copy of their work

Black Music History Q&A

Question:
What is Black Music?

Answer:
Black music is music created, produced, or inspired by black people, people of African descent.

Question:
What are some of the music genres that have been created by Black people in America ?

Answer:
African American music, Acid House, Bluegrass, Blues, Blues Rock, Bounce Music, Breakbeat, Chicago Blues, Chicago House, Country, Deep House, Detroit Blues, Detroit Techno, Contemporary, R&B, Disco, Doo-wop, Electric Blues, Electro Funk, Garage, Go-go, Gospel music, Hard Rock, Heavy Metal, Hip Hop, Hip House, House Jazz, Memphis Blues, Minimal Techno, Neo Soul, New Orleans Blues, Ragtime, Rap, Rhythm &Blues, Rock, Rock & Roll, Rockabilly, Soul, Spirituals, Swing, Techno, Texas Blues, Zydeco and more.

Question:
Is Black Music only created in America?

Answer:
No, Black music has been created all over the world in any place that Black people have ever lived.

Works Cited

Wikipedia contributors. (2021, October 23). African blues. In *Wikipedia, The Free Encyclopedia*. Retrieved 03:40, December 15, 2021, https://en.wikipedia.org/w/index.php?title=African_blues&oldid=1051502289

Wikipedia contributors. (2021, December 7). Blues. In *Wikipedia, The Free Encyclopedia*. Retrieved 03:42, December 15, 2021, https://en.wikipedia.org/w/index.php?title=Blues&oldid=1059108027

20th Century Music, https://www.pbs.org/opb/historydetectives/feature/20th-century-music/

Tauber, Allen. (2015), History Of The Djembe, Retrieved December 15, 2021, https://www.drumconnection.com/africa-connections/history-of-the-djembe/

Wikipedia contributors. (2021, December 12). Djembe. In *Wikipedia, The Free Encyclopedia*. Retrieved 04:31, December 15, 2021, https://en.wikipedia.org/w/index.php?title=Djembe&oldid=1059963023

Wikipedia contributors. (2021, December 12). Griot. In *Wikipedia, The Free Encyclopedia*. Retrieved 04:36, December 15, 2021, https://en.wikipedia.org/w/index.php?title=Griot&oldid=1059963326

Wikipedia contributors. (2022, January 22). Banjo. In *Wikipedia, The Free Encyclopedia*. Retrieved 07:47, February 2, 2022, https://en.wikipedia.org/w/index.php?title=Banjo&oldid=1067223461

Paul Ruta, February 16th, 2021, *A Quest to Return the Banjo to Its African Roots* https://www.smithsonianmag.com/blogs/smithsonian-center-folklife-cultural-heritage/2021/02/16/quest-return-banjo-its-african-roots/.

Wikipedia contributors. (2021, August 29). Ngoni (instrument). In *Wikipedia, The Free Encyclopedia*. Retrieved 04:46, December 15, 2021, https://en.wikipedia.org/w/index.php?title=Ngoni_(instrument)&oldid=1041182562

Words & Audio by Jenna Strucko, https://bittersoutherner.com/history-of-the-banjo#.YgP8iOrMK00

Featured Object: West African Ngoni, Author: Robin Kuprewicz, Post Date:2/3/2017 https://www.spurlock.illinois.edu/blog/p/featured-object-west/110

Wikipedia contributors. (2021, December 13). Hip hop music. In *Wikipedia, The Free Encyclopedia*. Retrieved 18:28, December 14, 2021, https://en.wikipedia.org/w/index.php?title=Hip_hop_music&oldid=1060179725

Wikipedia contributors. (2021, November 28). Afro–Latin Americans. In *Wikipedia, The Free Encyclopedia* Retrieved18:58December14,2021, https://en.wikipedia.org/w/index.php?title=Afro%E2%80%93Latin_Americans&oldid=1057604325

Wikipedia contributors. (2022, February 12). Black Hispanic and Latino Americans. In Wikipedia, The Free Encyclopedia. Retrieved 22:25, February 16, 2022, https://en.wikipedia.org/w/index.php?title=Black_Hispanic_and_Latino_Americans&oldid=1071349185

By Sounds and Colours , November 20, 2019, The History And Impact Of Latin American Music https://soundsandcolours.com/subjects/travel/the-history-and-impact-of-latin-american-music-49112/

Wikipedia contributors. (2021, December 10). Jazz. In *Wikipedia, The Free Encyclopedia*. Retrieved 19:01, December 14, 2021, https://en.wikipedia.org/w/index.php?title=Jazz&oldid=1059664849

The Origins of Jazz, https://jazzobserver.com/the-origins-of-jazz/

Wikipedia contributors. (2021, December 13). Rhythm and blues. In *Wikipedia, The Free Encyclopedia*. Retrieved 19:02, December 14, 2021, https://en.wikipedia.org/w/index.php?title=Rhythm_and_blues&oldid=1060014313

A Message From The Great Nina Simone, by Be Wise on January 28, 2013, in Everything Else, Historical Profiles, https://wisdomftf.com/2013/01/28/a-message-from-the-great-nina-simone/

The Pitch. Nina Simone's Insistent Blackness
Critic William C. Anderson on Nina Simone's enduring legacy and how she "commands her listeners as a Black woman." By William C. Anderson, July 27, 2015, https://pitchfork.com/thepitch/849-nina-simones-insistent-blackness/

Wikipedia contributors. (2021, December 9). Spirituals. In *Wikipedia, The Free Encyclopedia*. Retrieved 19:10, December 14, 2021, https://en.wikipedia.org/w/index.php?title=Spirituals&oldid=1059490621

Wikipedia contributors. (2021, July 5). Traditional black gospel. In *Wikipedia, The Free Encyclopedia*. Retrieved 16:33, January 30, 2022, https://en.wikipedia.org/w/index.php?title=Traditional_black_gospel&oldid=1032164687

Wikipedia contributors. (2022, January 13). Rock and roll. In *Wikipedia, The Free Encyclopedia*. Retrieved 05:01, February 2, 2022, https://en.wikipedia.org/w/index.php?title=Rock_and_roll&oldid=1065349108

Matt Stahl, Olufunmilayo Arewa, https://theconversation.com/denying-black-musicians-their-royalties-has-a-history-emerging-out-of-slavery-144397

Wikipedia contributors. (2022, January 22). Black music. In *Wikipedia, The Free Encyclopedia*. Retrieved 17:54, February 8, 2022, https://en.wikipedia.org/w/index.php?title=Black_music&oldid=1067241792

Wikipedia contributors. (2021, April 17). List of musical genres of the African diaspora. In *Wikipedia, The Free Encyclopedia*. Retrieved 18:24, February 8, 2022, https://en.wikipedia.org/w/index.php?title=List_of_musical_genres_of_the_African_diaspora&oldid=1018408574

www.ingramcontent.com/pod-product-compliance
Lightning Source LLC
Chambersburg PA
CBHW032128090426
42743CB00007B/514